AF489373

LET'S EXPLORE SOUTH AMERICA

(MOST FAMOUS ATTRACTIONS IN SOUTH AMERICA)

BABY PROFESSOR

EDUCATION KIDS

Speedy Publishing LLC
40 E. Main St. #1156
Newark, DE 19711
www.speedypublishing.com

Copyright 2018

All Rights reserved. No part of this book may be reproduced or used in any way or form or by any means whether electronic or mechanical, this means that you cannot record or photocopy any material ideas or tips that are provided in this book.

South America occupies the southern portion of the Americas. South America is one of the most biodiverse continents on earth.

Machu Picchu
is located in the
Cusco Region,
Urubamba Province,
Machupicchu
District in Peru.
The Incas built the
estate around 1450,
but abandoned
it a century later
at the time of the
Spanish Conquest.

Angel Falls is the world's highest uninterrupted waterfall. Angel Falls is located in the Canaima National Park. Angel Falls is one of Venezuela's top tourist attractions.

Christ the Redeemer is the largest art deco statue in the world. The statue is located in the Tijuca Forest National Forest, at the top of the Corcovado Mountain. The statue has become an icon for Rio de Janeiro and Brazil.

Lake Titicaca is located on the south eastern part of Peru and on the western part of Bolivia. It is the largest lake in South America. It is often called the highest navigable lake in the world.

The Galápagos Islands are an archipelago of volcanic islands that span across the equator line. The most famous of the endemic Galapagos creatures are the tortoises that the islands were named after.

Easter Island is a Polynesian island in the Pacific Ocean. Easter Island is famous for its 887 extant monumental statues, called moai, created by the early Rapa Nui people.

Torres del Paine
National Park is
a national park
encompassing
mountains, glaciers,
lakes, and rivers in
southern Chilean
Patagonia. The
national park is
a popular hiking
destination.

www.ingramcontent.com/pod-product-compliance
Lightning Source LLC
Chambersburg PA
CBHW060151120726
48003CB00010B/3107